First Facts™

Positively Pets

Caring for Your Hamster

by Adele Richardson

Consultant:
Jennifer Zablotny, DVM
Member, American Veterinary Medical Association

Capstone
press®
Mankato, Minnesota

First Facts is published by Capstone Press,
151 Good Counsel Drive, P.O. Box 669, Mankato, Minnesota 56002.
www.capstonepress.com

Library of Congress Cataloging-in-Publication Data
Richardson, Adele, 1966–
     Caring for your hamster / Adele Richardson.
     p. cm. —(First facts. Positively pets)
     Summary: "Describes caring for a hamster, including supplies needed, feeding, cleaning,
health, safety, and aging"—Provided by publisher.
     Includes bibliographical references and index.
     ISBN-13: 978-0-7368-6387-2 (hardcover)
     ISBN-10: 0-7368-6387-7 (hardcover)
     1. Hamsters as pets—Juvenile literature. I. Title. II. Series.
SF459.H3R53 2007
636.9'356—dc22   2005035852

Editorial Credits
Becky Viaene, editor; Bobbi J. Wyss, designer; Kim Brown, illustrator; Kelly Garvin,
     photo researcher/photo editor

Photo Credits
Ardea/Johan de Meester, 14; John Daniels, 11
Capstone Press/Karon Dubke, cover (girl), 5, 6, 8–9, 12–13, 21
Norvia Behling, 7
Peter Arnold, Inc./KLEIN, 18
Photodisc, cover (hamster)
Shutterstock/James M. Phelps Jr., 20; Johanna Goodyear, 17

Capstone Press thanks Pet Expo, Mankato, Minnesota, for their assistance with this book.

1 2 3 4 5 6 11 10 09 08 07 06

Table of Contents

So You Want to Own a Hamster? 4

Supplies to Buy 6

Your Hamster at Home 8

Feeding Your Hamster 10

Cleaning 12

Hamster Health 15

Hamster Safety 16

Your Hamster's Life 19

Wild Relatives! 20

Decode Your Hamster's Behavior 21

Glossary 22

Read More 23

Internet Sites 23

Index 24

So You Want to Own a Hamster?

Hamsters crawl quickly inside their cages at the pet store. You want to take one of the hamsters home. But these small pets are a big **responsibility**.

Learn how to care for a hamster before you get one. Good care will help keep your hamster healthy.

I don't like to share my cage. If you put other hamsters in my cage, I'll fight with them.

GO AW

DWARF HAMSTER $19.99

5

Supplies to Buy

Most people buy hamsters and supplies at pet stores. Hamsters need cages or covered **aquariums**. They also need food, water bottles, and **bedding**.

Hamsters stay busy with toys.
They like to explore tubes in their
cages. Exercise wheels and chew
toys are also fun for hamsters.

Your Hamster at Home

Don't be surprised if your hamster is shy at first. Talk softly to your hamster. Let it sniff your hand every day. That's how your hamster will get to know you. After three or four days, try to gently pick it up.

Feeding Your Hamster

Your hungry hamster stuffs its big cheeks full of food. Hamsters eat early each evening. Make sure your pet always has plenty of hamster food and fresh water.

Each day, give your hamster a treat. Fresh fruit and vegetables, like small pieces of broccoli and apples, are safe treats.

Cleaning

Hamsters spend lots of time licking their fur. This is how they take a bath. You don't have to wash your hamster. But you do have to wash its cage. Every week, clean the cage with warm, soapy water and add new bedding.

Hamster Health

You can help your hamster stay healthy by giving it an exercise wheel. But even healthy hamsters sometimes get sick.

If your hamster stops eating or playing, take it to a **veterinarian**. The vet will tell you how to care for your sick pet.

15

Hamster Safety

You can safely play with your hamster outside of its cage. Hold the hamster in your hand. Or let your furry friend roll around in a clear plastic ball for a few minutes.

Hamsters should always be kept away from other pets. A dog or cat can hurt or kill a curious hamster.

Never let me run loose. I could get lost, sick, or hurt. I may even try to chew on furniture or wires.

18

Your Hamster's Life

Most hamsters live two or three years. Enjoy the time you have together. Exercise, good food, and a clean cage will help keep your hamster healthy. As your hamster gets older, it will sleep more and play less.

Wild Relatives!

You've probably noticed your hamster does a lot of chewing. That's because it's a **rodent**. Rodents have four front teeth that never stop growing. Squirrels, rats, and beavers are rodents too. Your hamster and its wild relatives chew on things to keep their teeth short.

Decode Your Hamster's Behavior

- Hamsters make squeaking sounds when they are frustrated, hurt, or sick.

- Hamsters fold their ears back and partly close their eyes when they're ready to sleep or just waking up. Be careful—sleepy hamsters are more likely to bite.

- Hamsters stretch and yawn when they are content.

- Hamsters fill the pouches in their cheeks with large amounts of food. This is how they move their food to different areas of the cage.

Glossary

aquarium (uh-KWAIR-ee-uhm)—a glass tank where pets, including hamsters, hermit crabs, and fish, are kept

bedding (BED-ing)—material used to make a bed; hamsters use wood shavings and shredded paper for bedding.

responsibility (ri-spon-suh-BIL-uh-tee)—a duty or a job

rodent (ROHD-uhnt)—a mammal with long front teeth used for gnawing; hamsters, rats, squirrels, and beavers are rodents.

veterinarian (vet-ur-uh-NER-ee-uhn)—a doctor who treats sick or injured animals; veterinarians also help animals stay healthy.

Read More

Ganeri, Anita. *Hamsters.* A Pet's Life. Chicago: Heinemann, 2003.

Hibbert, Clare. *Hamster.* Looking After Your Pet. North Mankato, Minn.: Smart Apple Media, 2005.

Nelson, Robin. *Pet Hamster.* First Step Nonfiction. Minneapolis: Lerner, 2003.

Internet Sites

FactHound offers a safe, fun way to find Internet sites related to this book. All of the sites on FactHound have been researched by our staff.

Here's how:

1. Visit *www.facthound.com*

2. Choose your grade level.

3. Type in this book ID **0736863877** for age-appropriate sites. You may also browse subjects by clicking on letters, or by clicking on pictures and words.

4. Click on the **Fetch It** button.

FactHound will fetch the best sites for you!

Index

behavior, 4, 8, 10, 12, 20, 21

chewing, 16, 20
cleaning, 12

exercising, 7, 15, 19

feeding, 10

health, 15

relatives, 20

sleeping, 19, 21

supplies, 4, 6, 7, 10, 12, 15, 16, 19, 21
    aquariums or cages, 4, 6, 7, 12, 15, 16, 19, 21
    bedding, 6, 12
    exercise wheels, 7, 15
    food, 6, 10, 19, 21
    water bottles, 6

toys, 7, 15, 16

veterinarians, 15

with other pets, 16